TRICK ORIGAMI

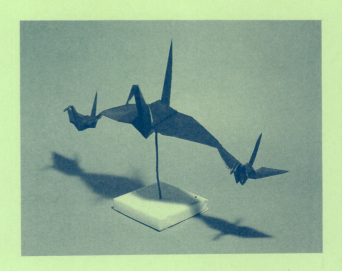

YOSHIHIDE MOMOTANI

© Copyright in Japan 1994 by Yoshihide Momotani

English text by Lauren Ollsin

Published by Seibundo Shinkosha Publishing Co., Ltd.
13-7, Yayoicho 1-chome, Nakano-ku, Tokyo, 164 Japan

Distributors:
UNITED STATES: *Kodansha America, Inc., through Farrar, Straus & Giroux, 19 Union Square West, New York, NY 10003.*
CANADA: *Fitzhenry & Whiteside Ltd., 195 Alistate Parkway, Markham, Ontario L3R 4T8.*
BRITISH ISLES AND EUROPEAN CONTINENT: *Premier Book Marketing Ltd., 1 Gower Street, London WC1E 6HA.*
AUSTRALIA AND NEW ZEALAND: *Bookwise International, 54 Crittenden Road, Findon, South Australia 5023.*
THE FAR EAST AND JAPAN: *Japan Publications Trading Co., Ltd., 1-2-1, Sarugaku-cho, Chiyoda-ku, Tokyo 101.*

First edition: July 1994

ISBN 0-87040-929-8

Printed in Japan

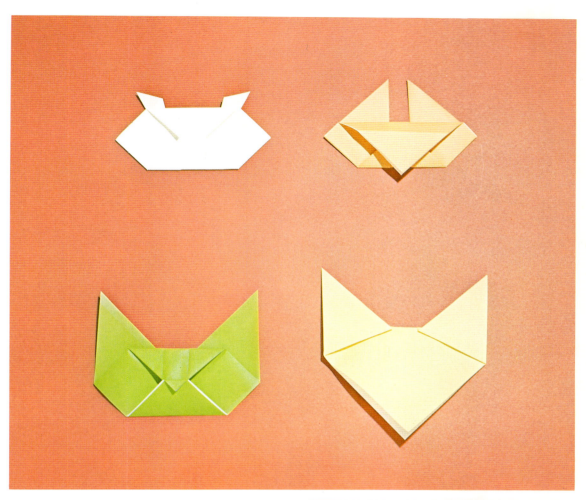

Piglet/Racoon
Cat/Fox

Chomp！(above) and
Talking Frogs (below)

Self-opening Flowers

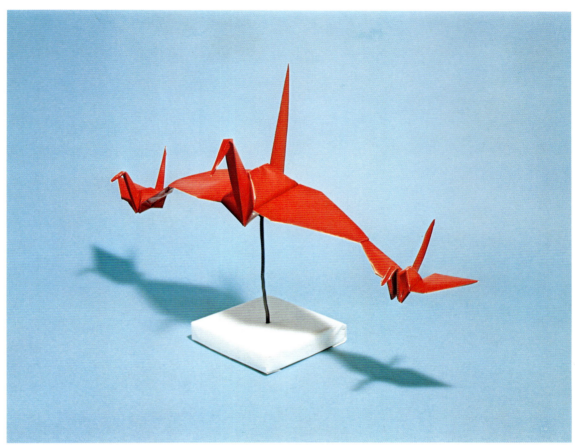

Crane Balancing Toy

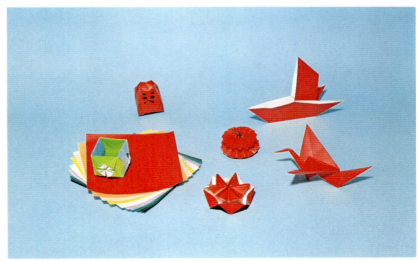

Trick Tools

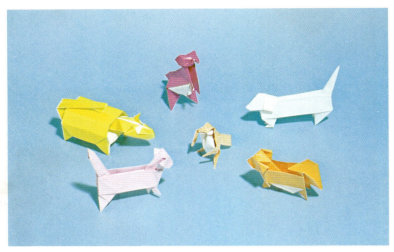

Various Animals

Frogs/Fish/Turtles

Paper Airplanes

PREFACE

Everyone wants to know some magic trick that no one else knows. Tricks that are written in books, or that you've learned from somebody else are probably not only not new, but chances are other people already know them. So, even if you read a book of trick ideas and learn how to do some of them, it might not amount to much.

When writing this book, I was troubled by this thought more than anything else. Also, if a person buys a book of trick origami thinking, "Okay, now I'm really going to do some magic tricks!" and their friends know about it beforehand, they may not meet with much success. Rather than just showing how to do tricks, I approached this book wanting to let people know that it is possible to come up with new tricks using origami.

Of course some of the examples are shown just as they have been done for generations, but it would give me great satisfaction to know that people who read this book apply the tricks in ways that only they know. That makes it all far more interesting.

Since its origins, origami has been an art in which all kinds of different things can be made from a single sheet of paper. That in itself is quite a trick! In Japan however, where everyone is familiar with origami, it is not such an unusual thing, and is not really considered a trick at all. However, people living outside of Japan can still enjoy the fun of showing origami to people who have rarely or never seen it before.

The first chapter of this book deals with a variety of transformable origami. The second chapter introduces moving and talking origami, which is not just a matter of showing the shape, but also of describing what to do with it once it is made. Chapter 3 discusses some important basic points about doing tricks, such as the need to develop an element of surprise. As a result, the actual number of examples in Chapter 3 are quite few.

Shapes made with origami have always been rather abstract looking. Chapter 4 explains some simple devices to help origami better resemble whatever it has been modeled after, plus some ways of adding to traditional designs passed down from long ago. I encourage you to apply these ideas in all kinds of ways to come up with your own new origami creations. Chapter 5 introduces the principles of flight and balance.

This book includes several origami that have been around for literally ages. Please remember that when people in olden times thought up some new origami, they naturally used subject matter from their era. So in the same way, since simply passing along tried and true patterns is not terribly exciting, I encourage you to modernize them, and make things that are interesting to you in terms of your own present time in history.

Contents

Contents

Origami Methods and Symbols

(some common examples)

— — — — — — — — This line shows a concave fold and is called a valley fold.

This shows the direction to move the paper being folded.

Example:

| 1 | 2 | 3 | 4 | 5 | 6 | 7 |

Steps 2 to 6 are viewed from a side angle.

In this book, generally only the first and last diagrams are shown, with mid-steps like 2 to 6 being omitted.

1/3 This mark at the creaseline means fold one third of the paper. If the paper is obviously being folded in half, nothing special is written.

— — — — — — — This line shows a convex fold, called a mountain fold.

This shows the direction of paper folded away from the fold line, becoming hidden on the other side. Note the shape of the arrowhead.

Example:

| 1 | 2 | 3 | 4 | 5 | 6 |

Steps 2 to 5 are viewed from a side angle.

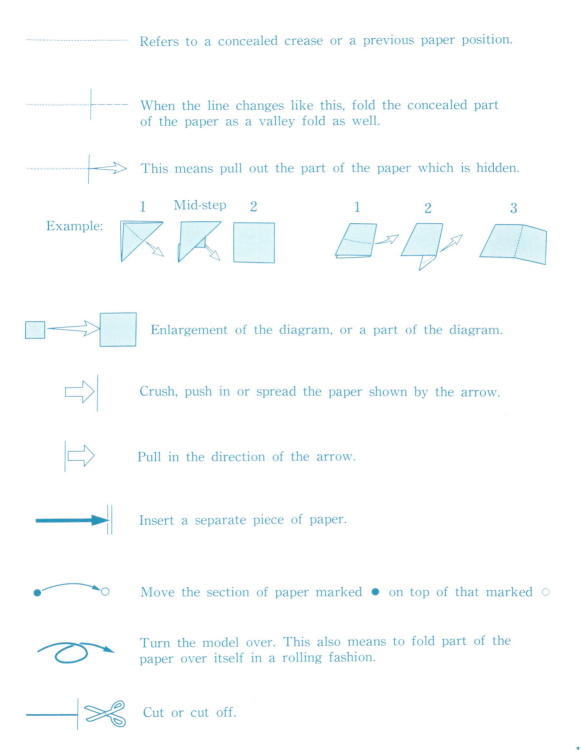

Refers to a concealed crease or a previous paper position.

When the line changes like this, fold the concealed part of the paper as a valley fold as well.

This means pull out the part of the paper which is hidden.

Example:

1   Mid-step   2   1   2   3

Enlargement of the diagram, or a part of the diagram.

Crush, push in or spread the paper shown by the arrow.

Pull in the direction of the arrow.

Insert a separate piece of paper.

Move the section of paper marked ● on top of that marked ○

Turn the model over. This also means to fold part of the paper over itself in a rolling fashion.

Cut or cut off.

Inside Reverse Fold

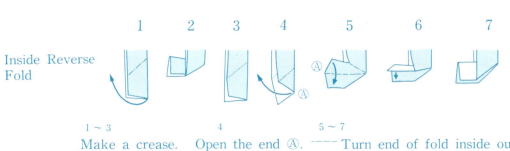

1 ~ 3	4	5 ~ 7
Make a crease.	Open the end Ⓐ.	----- Turn end of fold inside out and close.

Outside Reverse Fold

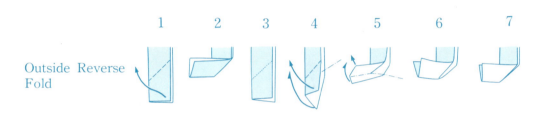

In this book, only the first and last diagrams are shown.

Stairstep Fold

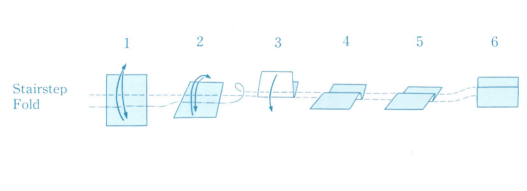

Crimp

1   Mid-step   2

Transforming Tricks

One of the origami designs which has been around for ages is the "Deceptive Boat" (see page 14). The shape of the hull and the sail are the same, so even if hull and sail change positions, it looks like the same boat. It becomes a trick because it looks the same even when the folds have been changed. The same is true for "Changing Ghost Pictures" and the "Kuridashi" too.

Furthermore, the characteristics of origami are really apparent in the piglet, racoon, fox and cat fold and refold combination (page 19). In this case, various ears and noses are added to a triangular face in different combinations to recreate various animals. If we think about the shape of the face and the parts to be added around the edge, we can create just about anything we like in the way of new origami.

Deceptive Boat

This origami trick is one that has been passed down through the ages.

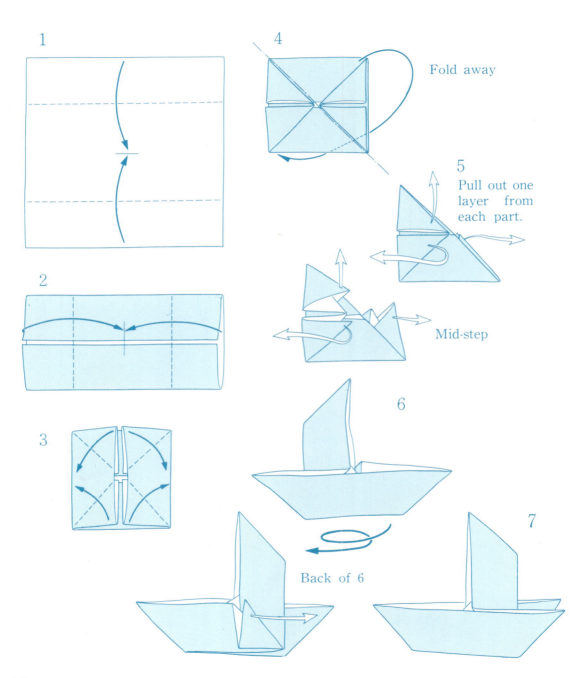

1

2

3

4

Fold away

5

Pull out one layer from each part.

Mid-step

6

Back of 6

7

How to do the trick

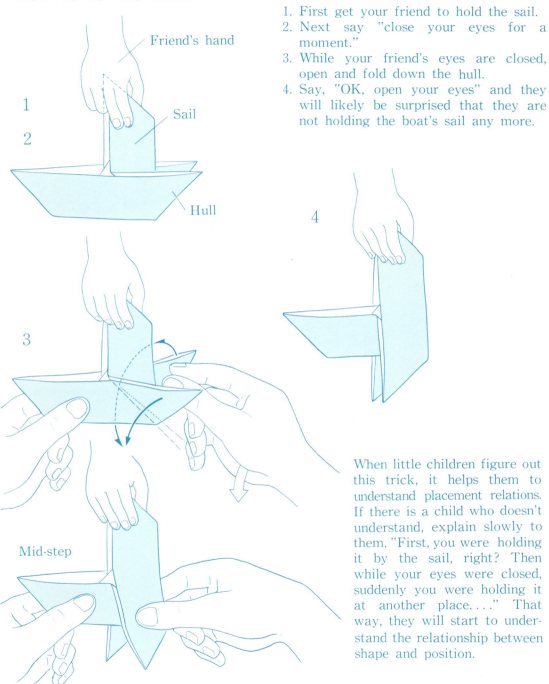

Friend's hand

Sail

Hull

1

2

3

Mid-step

4

1. First get your friend to hold the sail.
2. Next say "close your eyes for a moment."
3. While your friend's eyes are closed, open and fold down the hull.
4. Say, "OK, open your eyes" and they will likely be surprised that they are not holding the boat's sail any more.

When little children figure out this trick, it helps them to understand placement relations. If there is a child who doesn't understand, explain slowly to them, "First, you were holding it by the sail, right? Then while your eyes were closed, suddenly you were holding it at another place...." That way, they will start to understand the relationship between shape and position.

Origami made by refolding

This origami has also been made since long ago.

Catamaran

1   This is the sailboat from the last page.

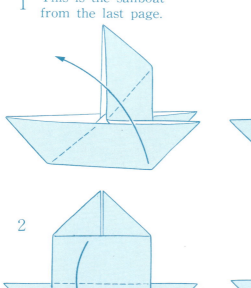

2

3

4

Windmill

1   This is step 2 on the left

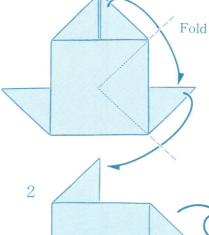

Fold

2

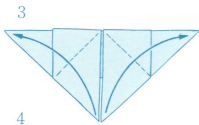
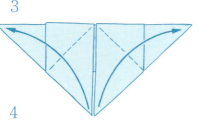

5   Finished

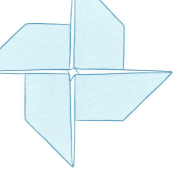

Looks like a flower just like this, but can be a windmill if you pierce it with a stick.

Butterfly

Flower A

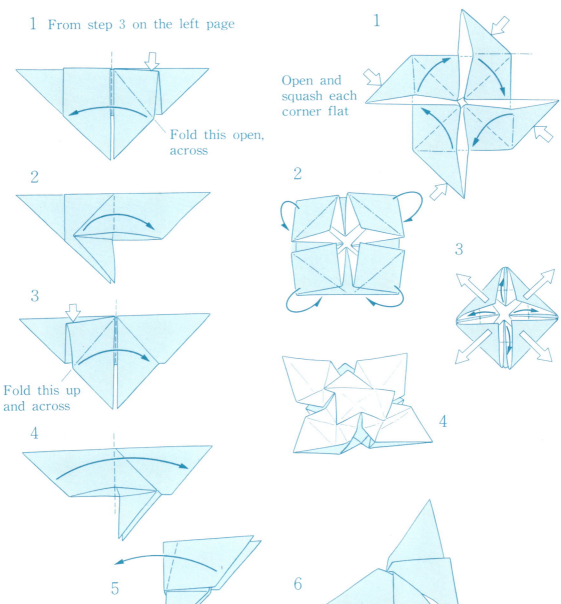

Butterfly

1 From step 3 on the left page

Fold this open, across

2

3

Fold this up and across

4

5

Flower A

From Windmill on previous page

1

Open and squash each corner flat

2

3

4

6

Finished butterfly

Animal Faces

This is a multi-animal-face trick. First let's make the piglet face and after that we can fold and change it into other animals too.

Piglet

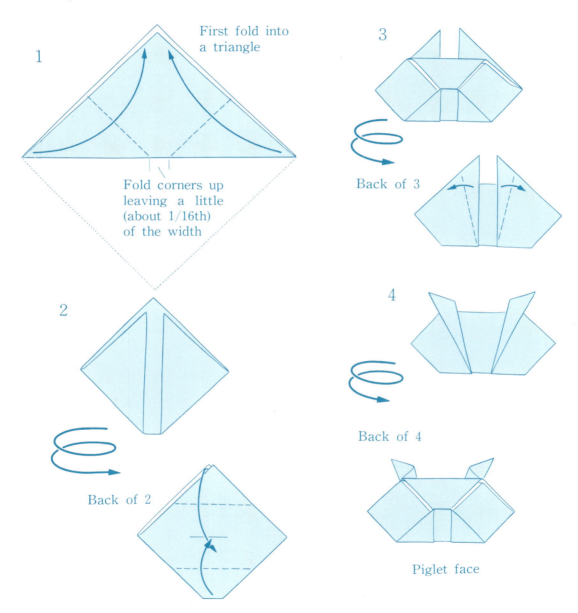

1

First fold into a triangle

Fold corners up leaving a little (about 1/16th) of the width

2

Back of 2

3

Back of 3

4

Back of 4

Piglet face

Piglet-Racoon-Fox-Cat

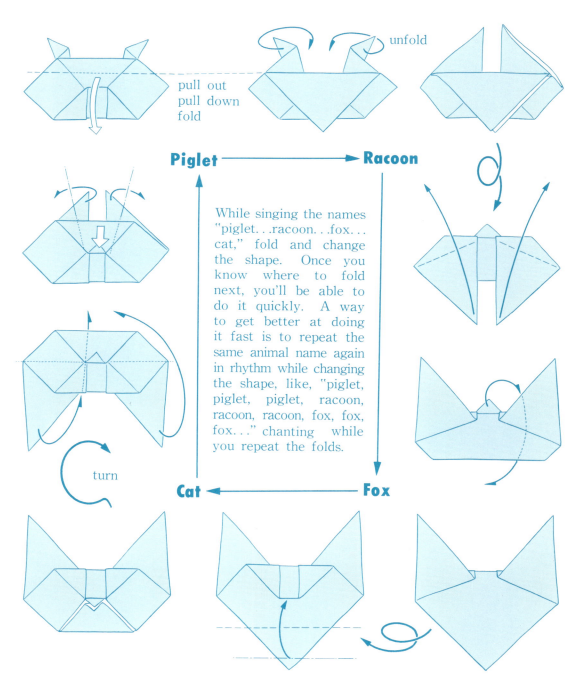

pull out
pull down
fold

unfold

Piglet ⟶ **Racoon**

While singing the names "piglet...racoon...fox... cat," fold and change the shape. Once you know where to fold next, you'll be able to do it quickly. A way to get better at doing it fast is to repeat the same animal name again in rhythm while changing the shape, like, "piglet, piglet, piglet, racoon, racoon, racoon, fox, fox, fox..." chanting while you repeat the folds.

turn

Cat ⟵ **Fox**

Changing Ghost Pictures

In this trick, draw pictures on the folded paper, and then as you move it, different pictures emerge.

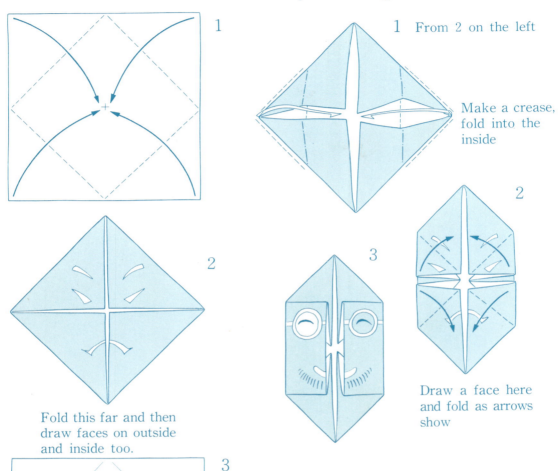

1

1 From 2 on the left

Make a crease, fold into the inside

2

2

3

Draw a face here and fold as arrows show

Fold this far and then draw faces on outside and inside too.

3

The number or combination of folds you make will change the face, and unlike the face on the left, you can change just part of it, too.

20

Kuridashi A

This method of folding, layering, opening up and refolding has been passed down through the ages. This is one example.

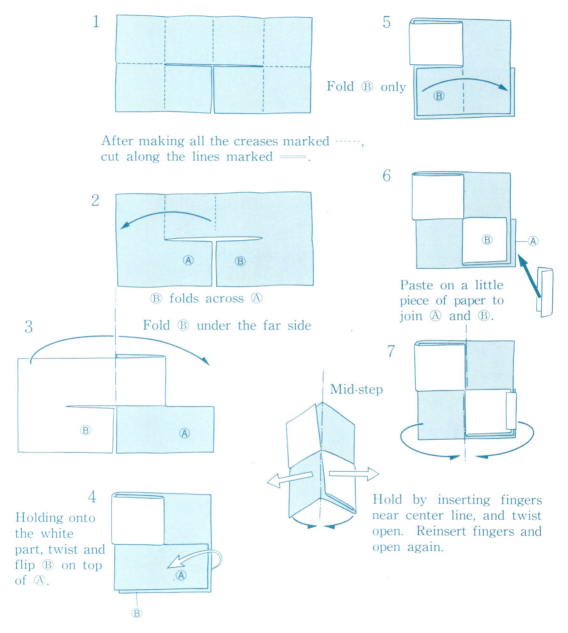

1

After making all the creases marked ------, cut along the lines marked ===.

2

Ⓑ folds across Ⓐ

Fold Ⓑ under the far side

3

4

Holding onto the white part, twist and flip Ⓑ on top of Ⓐ.

5

Fold Ⓑ only

6

Paste on a little piece of paper to join Ⓐ and Ⓑ.

Mid-step

7

Hold by inserting fingers near center line, and twist open. Reinsert fingers and open again.

Flower B

This flower is folded like the bellows of an oldfashioned camera or a lampshade.

1   Use strong paper that is about twice as wide as it is high.

2

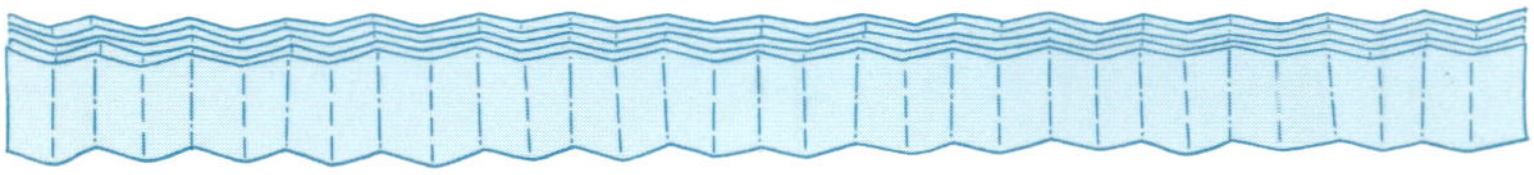

3 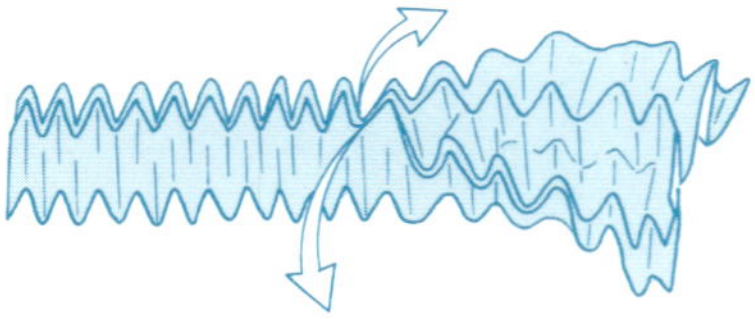   Pull the paper layers apart.    Side angle view of 4

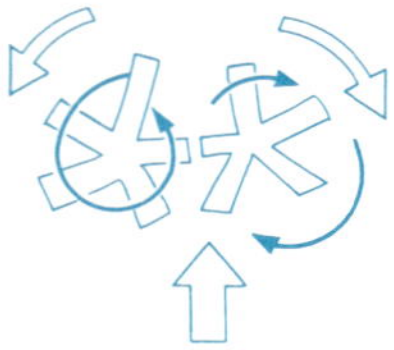

4 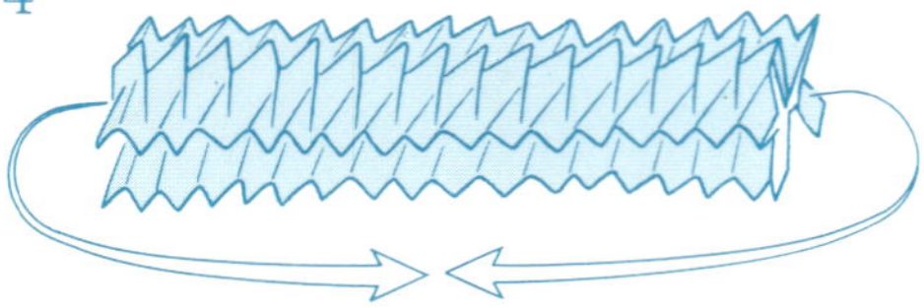   Connect both ends to make a ring.

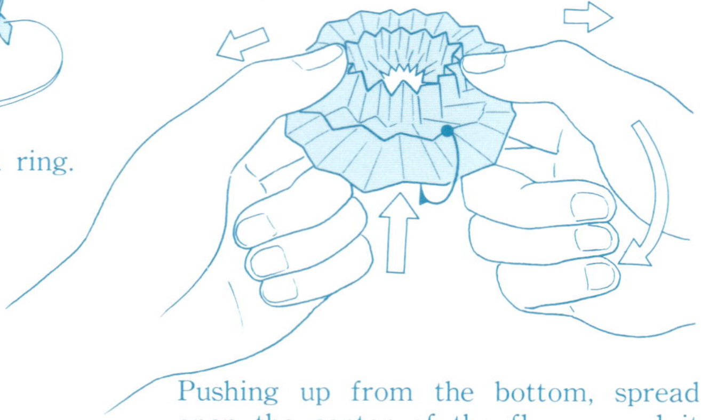

5

Finished

Pushing up from the bottom, spread open the center of the flower, and it will bloom forever.

Three-Dimensional Kuridashi

A variation on Flower B. Use paper that is slightly stiff and three times as wide as it is high. Make the creases, then allow criss-cross valley folds to pull in all the black dots.

1

2

Open up again.

3

Make new creases in the spaces between the other creases. Glue the right and left edges to make a cylinder at this paste-up margin.

4

Fold along the lines creased in 3

5

Gather all tightly in. Push up from the bottom, and you can turn it inside out again and again.

Kuridashi B

No one knows who first thought up this kind of origami that is turned inside out again and again, but in olden times, they were called "Kaleidoscopes" because of their lovely colors and were sold in shops.

How to fold

1 Use paper about 6 times as long as wide

2   Fold into an equilateral triangle

3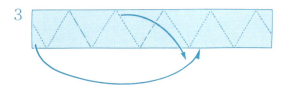

Playing With It

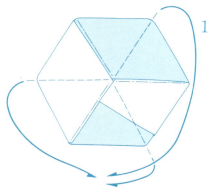

1

Fold away so that it gathers together

4 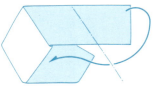 Fold under and lay on top of bottom part

Mid-step

Squish in at arrows. Open up center, turn inside out passing through hexagonal shape and repeat.

5  Attach here with glue

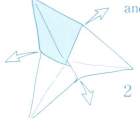

2

Moving and Talking Origami

"How could origami move?" you may be asking yourself. Well, the "Beak" is just an origami moving part. That's all it is. The wolf mouth "Chomp!" and the Talking Frog are made by attaching this moving part to the face. Though origami you can make some move by pulling on it, if you take a good look at it, and pull it in a completely different direction, you may well be able to make magic's element of surprise work for you.

Beak

Use paper that is a little bit stiff.

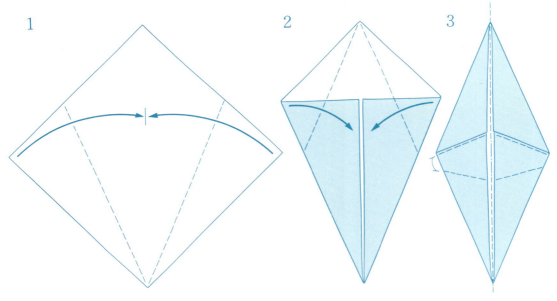

1

2

3

The top and bottom jaws are folded here.

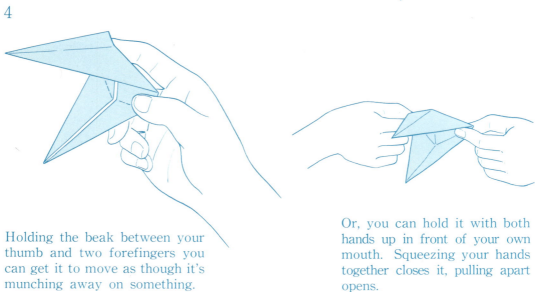

4

Holding the beak between your thumb and two forefingers you can get it to move as though it's munching away on something.

Or, you can hold it with both hands up in front of your own mouth. Squeezing your hands together closes it, pulling apart opens.

Champ ! !

This design uses the beak from the previous page. It's fun for scaring people with.

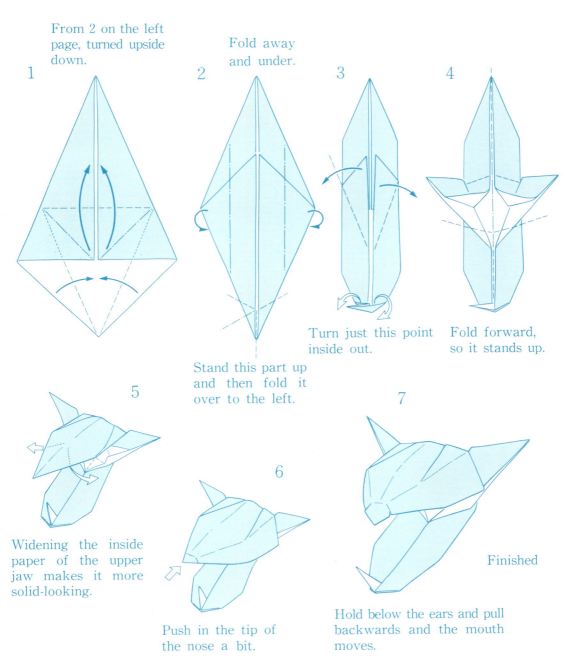

1 From 2 on the left page, turned upside down.

2 Fold away and under.

3 Turn just this point inside out.

4 Fold forward, so it stands up.

Stand this part up and then fold it over to the left.

5 Widening the inside paper of the upper jaw makes it more solid-looking.

6 Push in the tip of the nose a bit.

7 Finished

Hold below the ears and pull backwards and the mouth moves.

Talking Frog

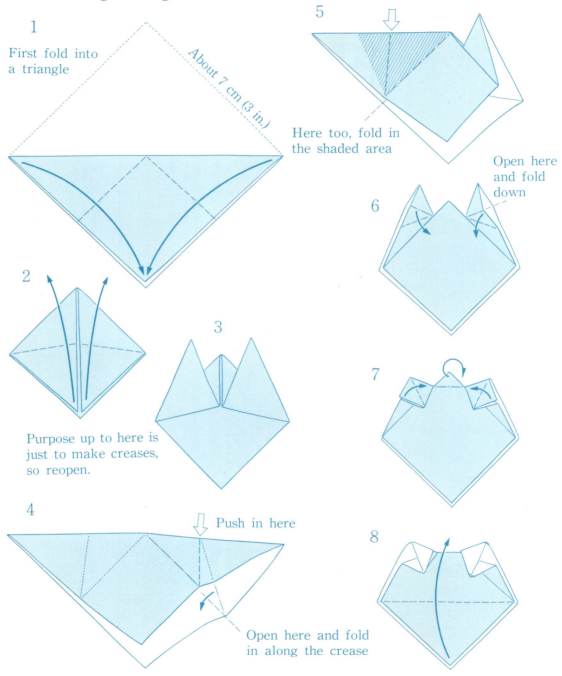

1

First fold into a triangle

About 7 cm (3 in.)

2

Purpose up to here is just to make creases, so reopen.

3

4

Push in here

Open here and fold in along the crease

5

Here too, fold in the shaded area

6

Open here and fold down

7

8

9

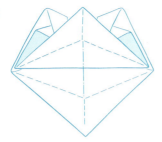

Fold and stand up mouth here

10

Fold backwards a bit

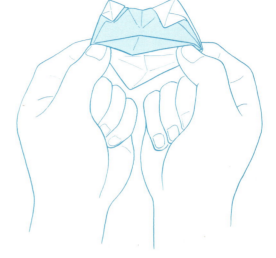

10 from the front

Hold firmly at the ● marks, bend the whole thing backwards a little, move back and forth firmly and the mouth will open. Keep doing that and the paper will start to make some sound, as though it is talking. In addition to this paper sound, you can say "ribbet, ribbet," or something like that to add depth to the sound.

The paper should not be too soft, should be dry, and one side should measure about 4 inches. The bigger the paper, the bigger the sound.

Jumping Frog

This frog jumps with just a little push from your finger!

1

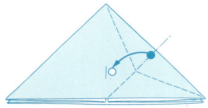

After you make these creases, move the parts marked ● to the ○ mark.

2

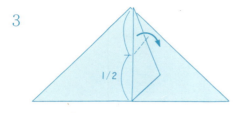

Note mountain fold at black dot.

3

1/2

4

Fold this the same as in 2 to 4

5

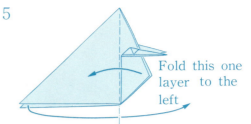

Fold this one layer to the left

Fold the far side to the right

6

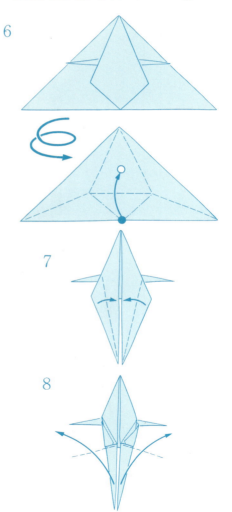

7

8

9

Enlargement

10

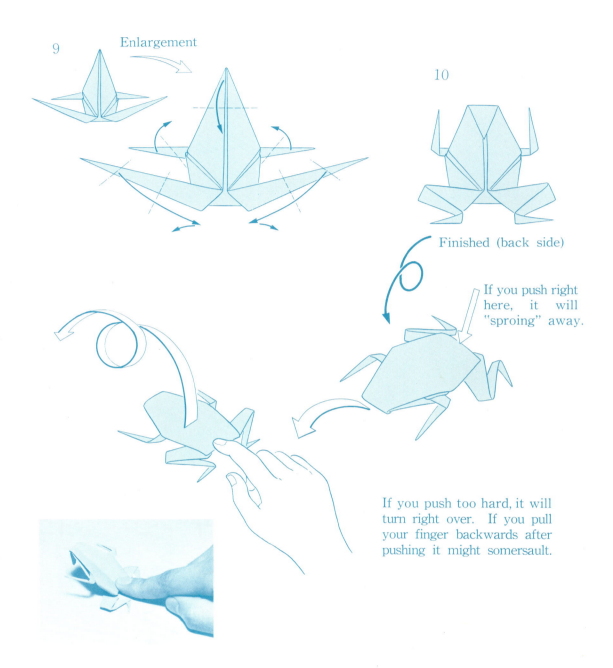

Finished (back side)

If you push right here, it will "sproing" away.

If you push too hard, it will turn right over. If you pull your finger backwards after pushing it might somersault.

Dharma Doll

This Dharma Doll can roll around and right itself.

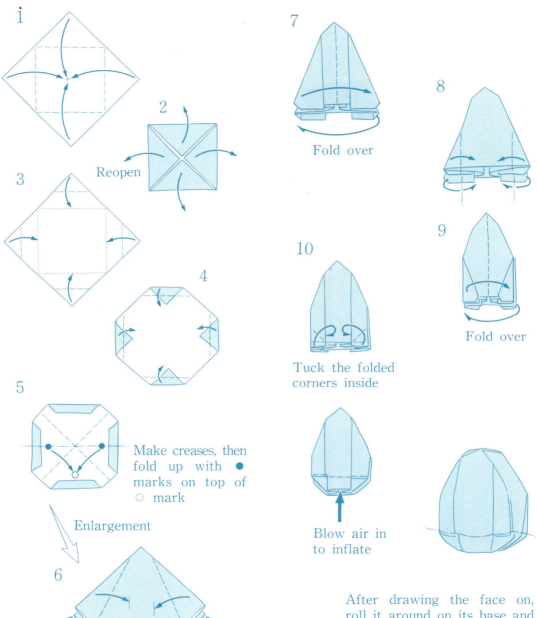

1

2 Reopen

3

4

5 Make creases, then fold up with ● marks on top of ○ mark

Enlargement

6 Fold the far side the same way

7 Fold over

8

9 Fold over

10 Tuck the folded corners inside

Blow air in to inflate

After drawing the face on, roll it around on its base and it should right itself automatically.

Flapping Wing Crane

This is one of many origami crane designs that have been passed down from generation to generation. The special feature of this one is that if you pull its tail, the wings flap.

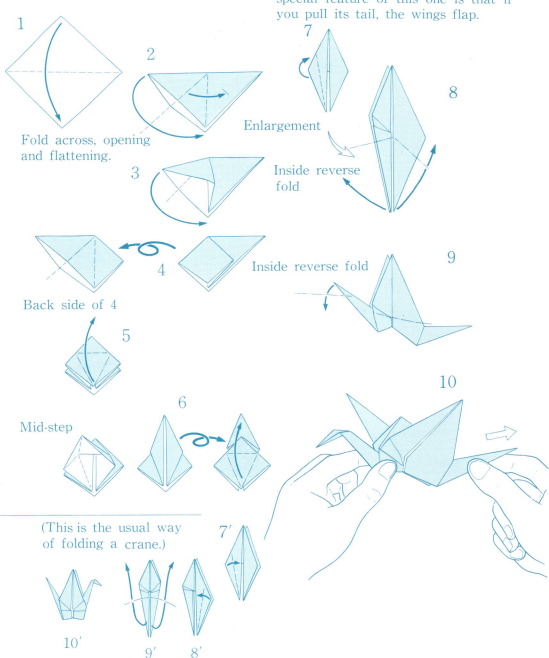

1

2

Fold across, opening and flattening.

3

4

Back side of 4

5

Mid-step

6

(This is the usual way of folding a crane.)

7'

9' 8'

10'

Enlargement

Inside reverse fold

Inside reverse fold

7

8

9

10

Japanese Racoon Dog/Tummy Drum

The Japanese racoon dog is a small Japanese animal a bit similar to the North American racoon, but without the distinctive striped markings. This origami is a combination of that animal and the small drum used in traditional music. It is a bit difficult to fold, so keep an eye on the diagrams. Use paper that is at least 20 cm (8 inches) wide.

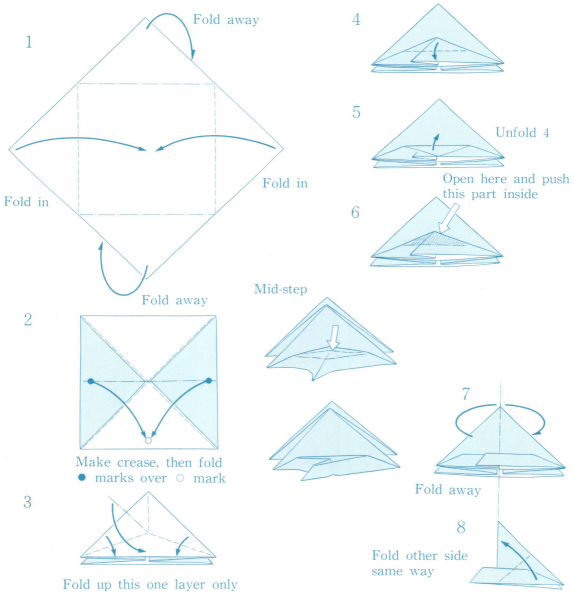

1
Fold away
Fold in
Fold in
Fold away

2
Make crease, then fold
● marks over ○ mark

3
Fold up this one layer only

4

5
Unfold 4
Open here and push this part inside

6

Mid-step

7
Fold away

8
Fold other side same way

34

9 Unfold this one layer and the same on the other side

10 From here on, always fold the far side the same

11 Outside reverse fold

12

13

14 Outside reverse fold

15 Inside reverse fold

Enlargement

16 Stairstep fold

17 Opening here a little, pull out the base of the tail so it points down

17' It's hard, but open here.

18' Puff out the head to look more solid

Pull the tail from here

18 Hold by the nape of the neck where the mark is and put your finger(s) inside to puff out the shape.

Hold at the neck mark and pull on the tail and the front legs should move.

19 Finished

Self-blooming Flower A

What would you think about an origami flower that opens on its own while you are asleep at night? The way this flower opens varies depending on the conditions, like the size and quality of paper you use, so it's a bit hard to predict. If you use typical Japanese origami paper spray water mist on the finished flower and within an hour or so it should open.

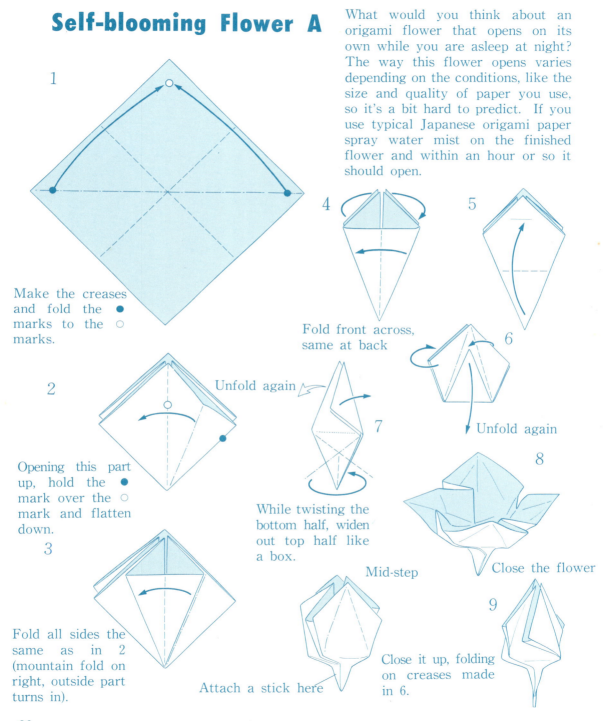

1

Make the creases and fold the ● marks to the ○ marks.

2

Opening this part up, hold the ● mark over the ○ mark and flatten down.

3

Fold all sides the same as in 2 (mountain fold on right, outside part turns in).

4

Fold front across, same at back

5

Unfold again

6

Unfold again

7

While twisting the bottom half, widen out top half like a box.

8

Close the flower

Mid-step

Attach a stick here

9

Close it up, folding on creases made in 6.

Self-blooming Flower B

This one, too, is folded into a bud that blooms when moistened with mist.

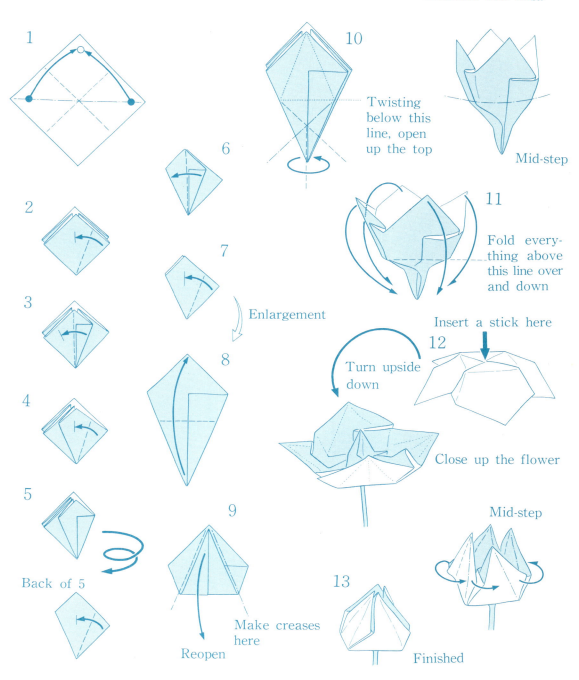

1

2

3

4

5

Back of 5

6

7

Enlargement

8

9

Make creases here

Reopen

10

Twisting below this line, open up the top

Mid-step

11

Fold every-thing above this line over and down

Turn upside down

Insert a stick here

12

Close up the flower

Mid-step

13

Finished

Paper Gun

This origami has also been around for ages. It makes a "Bang!" sound, but if the paper is too small, it won't make a sound at all. Use a big rectangular sheet of paper.

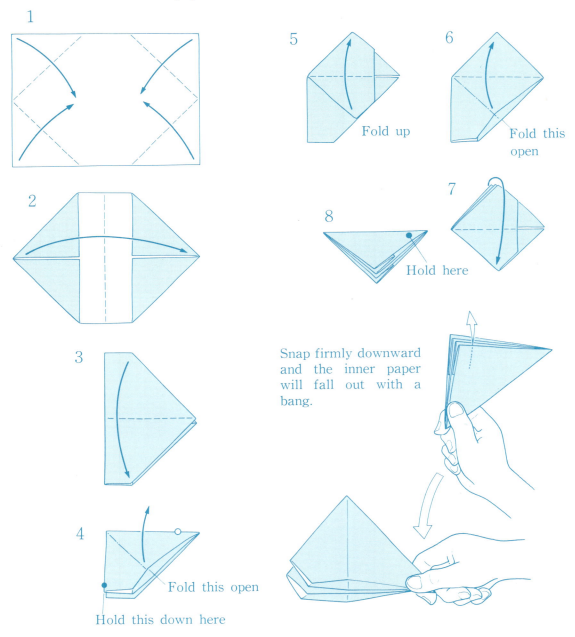

1

2

3

4

Fold this open

Hold this down here

5

Fold up

6

Fold this open

7

8

Hold here

Snap firmly downward and the inner paper will fall out with a bang.

A Hint About Magic

Seeing something unusual or experiencing something new often feels strange or surprising. The reason why Japanese people aren't surprised by origami is that they see it from the time they are young children. However, when non-Japanese people see origami for the first time, they are often quite surprised. Some people, who like to have everything proven or explained to them, won't rest until they have learned how to fold something themselves.

Sometimes creases and layers are used to create a three-dimensional effect. It makes it a lot easier to fold origami quickly when you have the creases already in place from the start. In this way too, if you unfold an origami you have made, folding it up a second time is a snap. The 10-second crane is made this way. As long as the creases are there, you can fold it so fast that people who don't know will think it's magic. In order to make this kind of trick work though, it's important to practice again and again so you really know which fold comes next. It is impressive simply because it goes against the belief that origami takes time to make.

One of the most important elements in doing magic tricks is to show something that seems to go contrary to common sense, and so I looked for designs with that quality to include in this book.

Möbius Ring (pronounced "may-be-us")

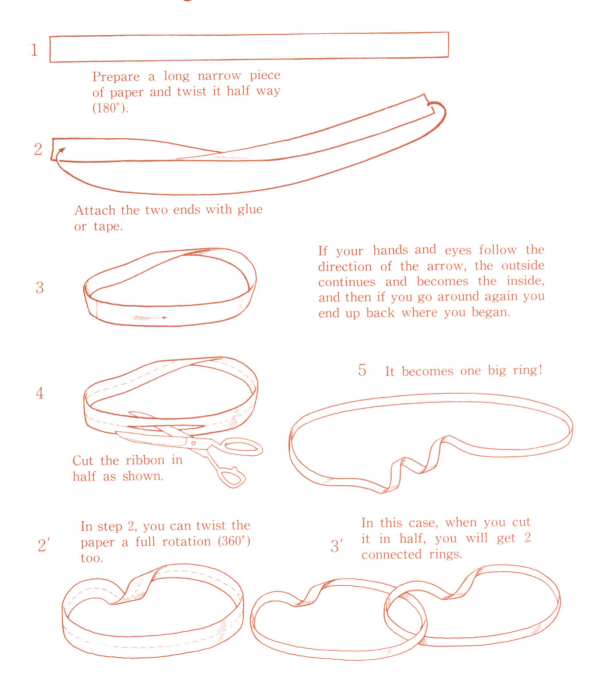

1 Prepare a long narrow piece of paper and twist it half way (180˚).

2 Attach the two ends with glue or tape.

3 If your hands and eyes follow the direction of the arrow, the outside continues and becomes the inside, and then if you go around again you end up back where you began.

4 Cut the ribbon in half as shown.

5 It becomes one big ring!

2' In step 2, you can twist the paper a full rotation (360˚) too.

3' In this case, when you cut it in half, you will get 2 connected rings.

Passing Through the Paper Hole

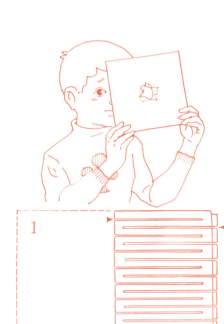

Do you think it's possible to pass through a hole cut in a small piece of paper?
Cut a hole in a small piece of paper then climb through it.
Do you think you can?
Cut your paper as in these next 3 steps, and you can easily pass through.

1

Fold the paper in half, then cut out the shape shown and unfold.

2 Leaving the two sides just as they are, cut along the dark line in the middle.

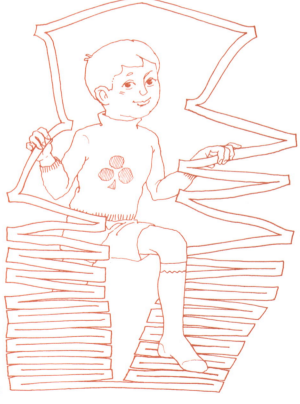

3 Stretch it out and it becomes a big hole.

The 10-Second Crane

Hint : make creases first

1

After making creases, fold the ● marks over the ○ mark.

2

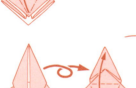

3

4

When you have made all of these folds firmly, you can leave the origami as it is in step 4 and then just before you amaze your friends with how fast you can do the 10-second crane, unfold it again.

With the creases folded in advance, it is much easier to make of course. And once the folds are there, you can change the folding order a bit too to add to the trick effect. With practice, you'll be able to fold it in 5 seconds. A good paper size for this is 10 to 14 inches (or 18 to 30 cm) square.

How to do the trick

1

Holding it lightly, shake it up and down.

Next change to hold it in the left hand.

2

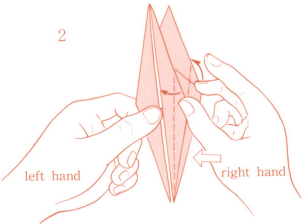

left hand   right hand

Folding with the thumb and middle finger of your right hand, put your left index finger inside.

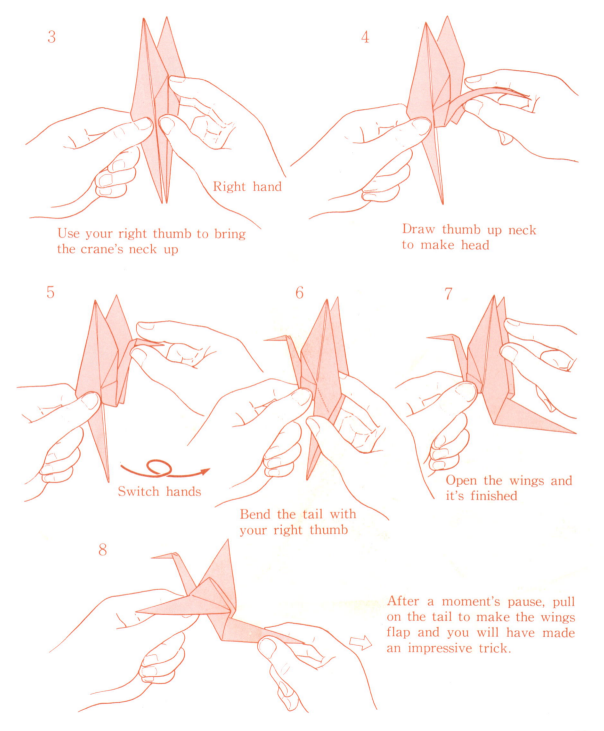

3

Right hand

Use your right thumb to bring
the crane's neck up

4

Draw thumb up neck
to make head

5

Switch hands

6

Bend the tail with
your right thumb

7

Open the wings and
it's finished

8

After a moment's pause, pull
on the tail to make the wings
flap and you will have made
an impressive trick.

43

Magical Box

Making boxes

You can put things in this box to make them disappear, and you can make decorative balls by joining 6 of these units together.

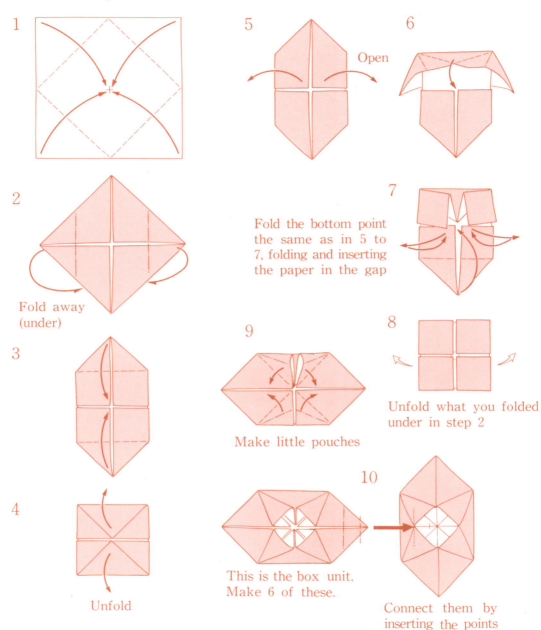

1

2

Fold away
(under)

3

4

Unfold

5

Open

6

7

Fold the bottom point
the same as in 5 to
7, folding and inserting
the paper in the gap

8

Unfold what you folded
under in step 2

9

Make little pouches

This is the box unit.
Make 6 of these.

10

Connect them by
inserting the points
and folding

Box Assembly

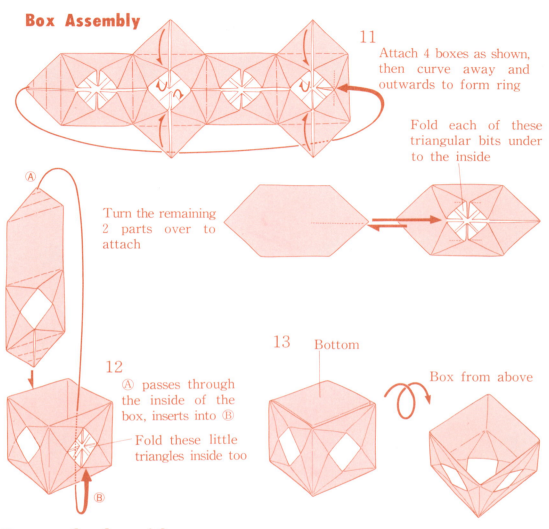

11 Attach 4 boxes as shown, then curve away and outwards to form ring

Fold each of these triangular bits under to the inside

Turn the remaining 2 parts over to attach

12 Ⓐ passes through the inside of the box, inserts into Ⓑ

Fold these little triangles inside too

13 Bottom

Box from above

How to do the trick You can also pull a scarf from an "empty" box.

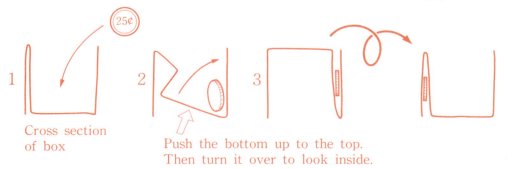

25¢

1 Cross section of box

2 Push the bottom up to the top. Then turn it over to look inside.

3

Turtle

With this one, no one can tell what it is until you finally pull it out into a 3-D turtle shape.

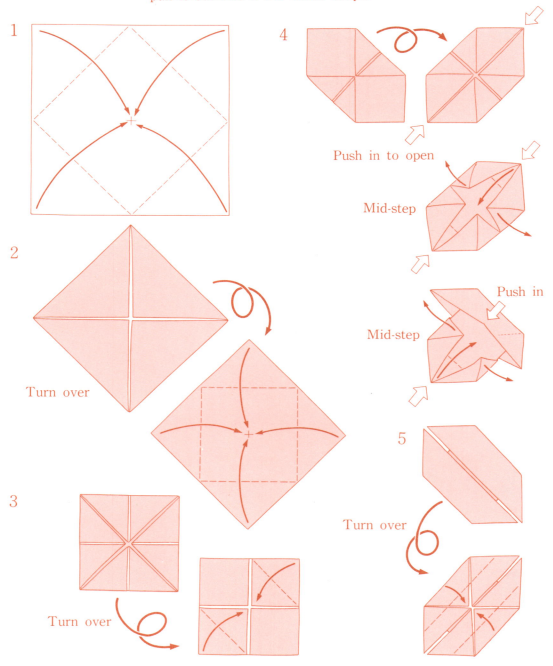

1

2

Turn over

3

Turn over

4

Push in to open

Mid-step

Mid-step

Push in

5

Turn over

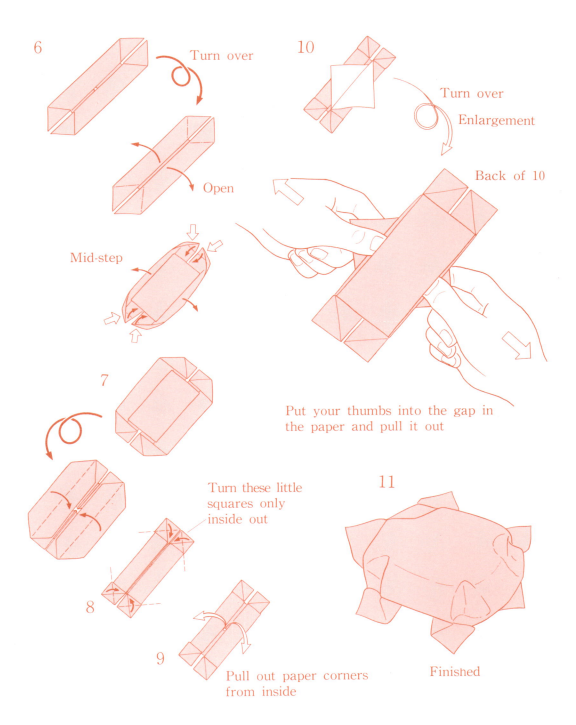

6

Turn over

Open

Mid-step

7

8

9

Turn these little
squares only
inside out

Pull out paper corners
from inside

10

Turn over

Enlargement

Back of 10

Put your thumbs into the gap in
the paper and pull it out

11

Finished

A trick to try....

It's fun to do tricks in which something suddenly disappears and reappears somewhere else. To do this kind of trick, it's extremely handy to have two of the same item. Of course, you can make a whole bunch of the same origami. To prepare for this trick, you make 2 of one origami, put one in your right pocket and have the other in your hand. And then...

Show your friend the one in your hand. Let them hold it.

When they hand it back to you, put it in your left pocket, then immediately pull out the one from your right pocket. This works as a trick in itself, but it is even better if we add a trick device along the way. Here is an example.

What to prepare:

A) A pile of origami paper. Turn it over, and then turn over just the top sheet so it's facing up. You also need a big handkerchief.

B) Two origami cranes, finished in the same color. Place one folded under the pile of paper and the other on top.

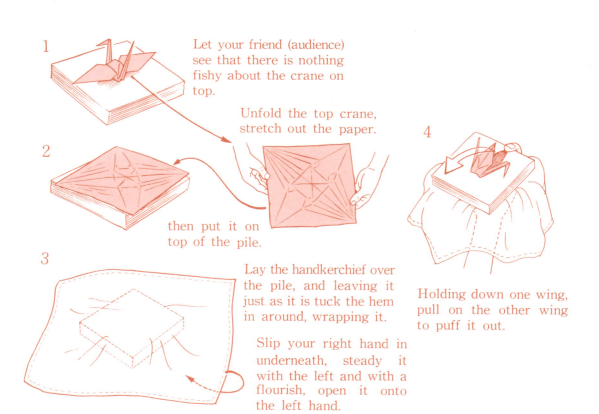

1 Let your friend (audience) see that there is nothing fishy about the crane on top.

Unfold the top crane, stretch out the paper.

2 then put it on top of the pile.

3 Lay the handkerchief over the pile, and leaving it just as it is tuck the hem in around, wrapping it.

Slip your right hand in underneath, steady it with the left and with a flourish, open it onto the left hand.

4 Holding down one wing, pull on the other wing to puff it out.

Just try folding something...

Generally speaking, a lot of simply made origami actually does resemble what it is modeled after, but sometimes when people are creating new origami designs this is not so. When a new origami is shown, even if the person who has made it thinks that it is obvious what it is, to other people it's not necessarily so clear.

One person looking at it might say, "Is this supposed to be a rabbit? It looks good!" The next person says, "No, isn't it a goldfish?" and then yet another says, "Hey, no, it's a chicken, isn't it?" which makes the person who made it stop and wonder what it really does look like.

Such being the case, to make things look more like the real thing, I have included some examples of how to improve the work without changing the basic traditional folding method. If you want to fold something in a simple way, it's important to first of all grasp the overall look of what you are trying to depict. Even if the folding becomes a little more complicated, ultimately you want to make something that truly represents your image. If you then fold it again and again using different types of paper and simplify it bit by bit, I think you need not end up saying, "So what does this look like, anyway?"

Crow

Anything that can be made in just 2 or 3 folds in itself seems like a magic trick just because it is so instant. A lot of these simply folded origami patterns are known from years gone by. However, sometimes it's hard to tell exactly what they are supposed to be!

This is just one example of origami that can be made precisely in a minimum of folds.

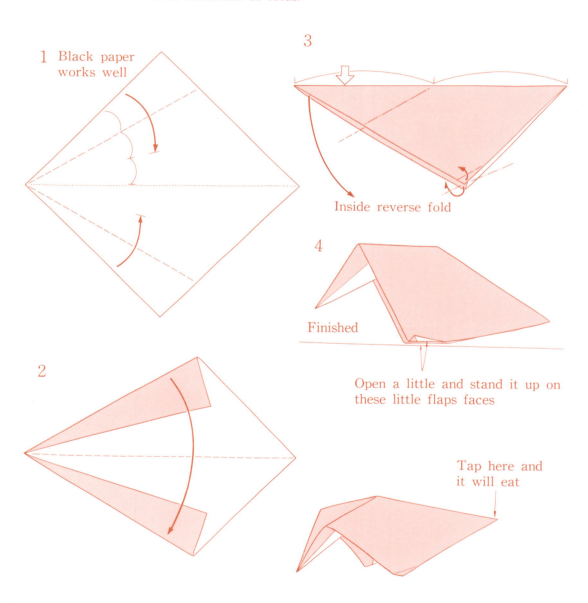

1 Black paper works well

2

3

Inside reverse fold

4

Finished

Open a little and stand it up on these little flaps faces

Tap here and it will eat

Monkey Face

Easy to fold. However, inflating it to look just right is a bit hard, so look closely at the diagrams.

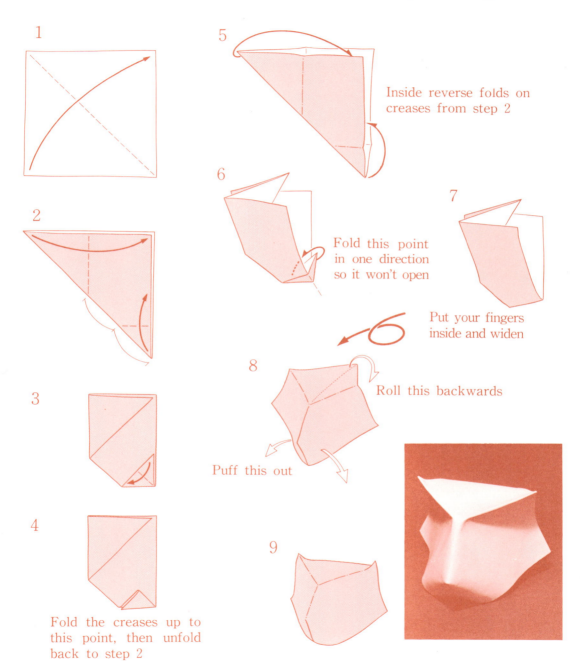

1

2

3

4

Fold the creases up to this point, then unfold back to step 2

5

Inside reverse folds on creases from step 2

6

Fold this point in one direction so it won't open

7

Put your fingers inside and widen

8

Roll this backwards

Puff this out

9

Basic Offering Box

Making a Sanbo

First make a "sanbo," a traditional table for placing offerings.   Then add little changes as you like.

1

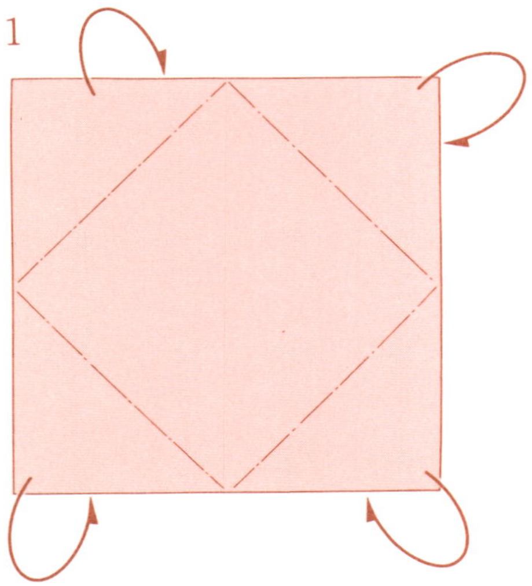

2

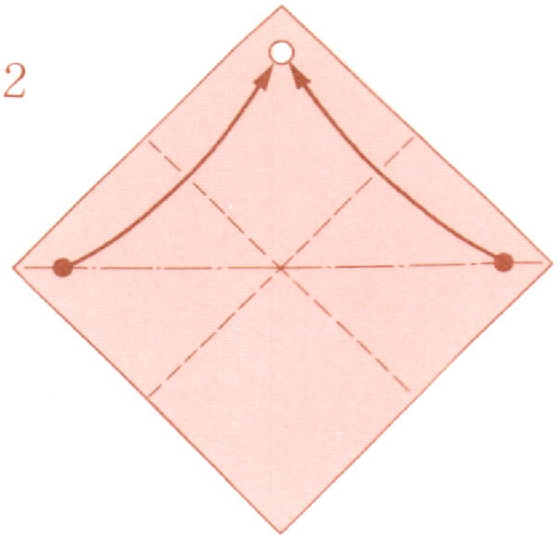

Make creases, then fold up

3

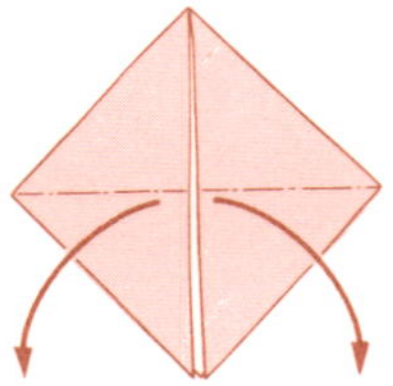

Fold open and down, front and back

4

Enlargement

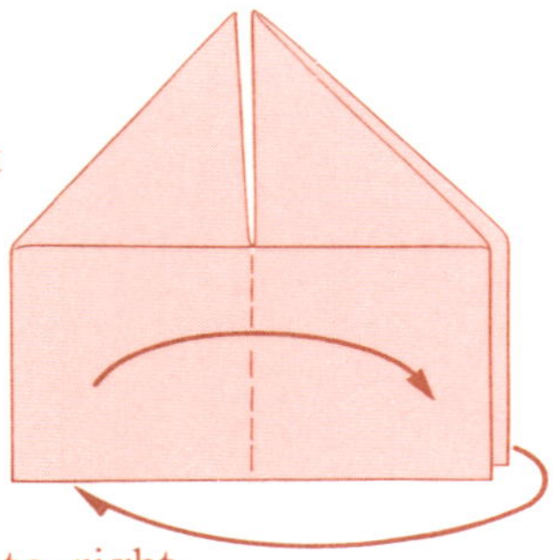

Fold front to right and back to left

5

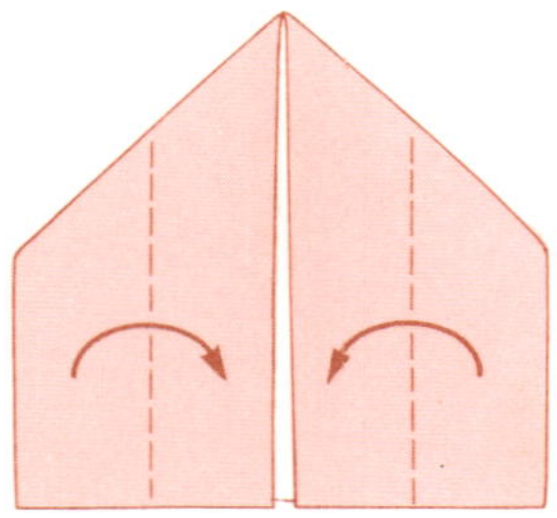

6

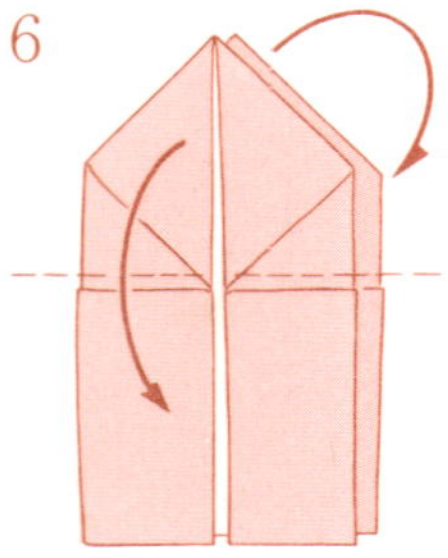

Spread the bottom out and it becomes a box

7

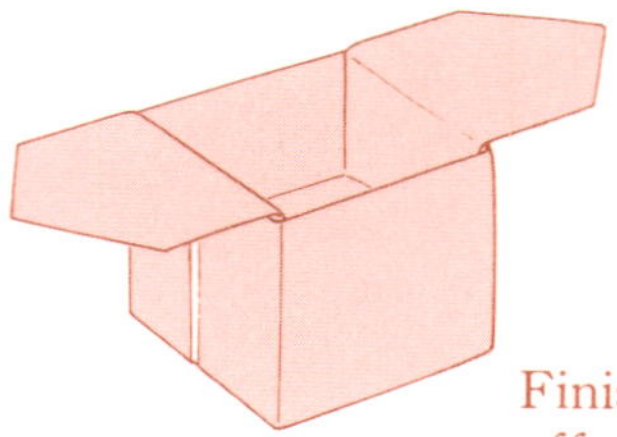

Finished "sanbo" offering table

Folding method used for various animals

Box for sweets (Sanbo with legs)

Another design passed down from olden times.

From step 4 on page 52

1

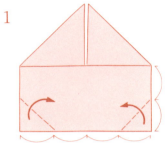

2

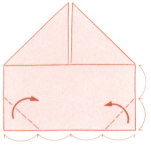

(Mountain)
Fold and tuck inside

3

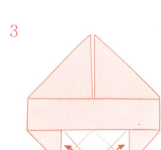

4

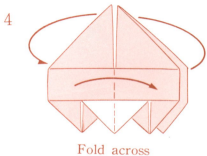

Fold across

5

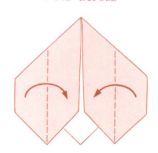

6

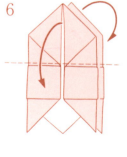

7

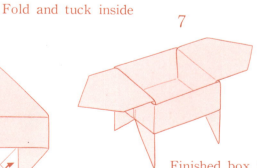

Finished box for
sweets or cakes

Puppy

Fold to step 7 on the previous page and then return the shape to step 6.

1′

Fold into the gap

2′

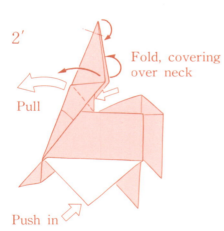

Fold, covering over neck

Pull

Push in

3′

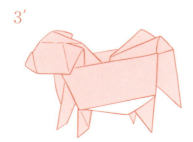

Long Dog

From step 7 on the last page

1″

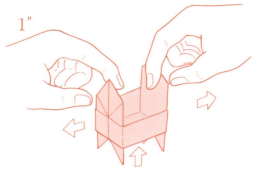

While pushing up the bottom, pull and stretch out

2″

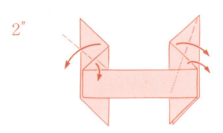

3″

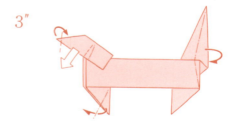

4″

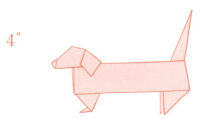

Flying Origami (Shape and Balance)

Here are some helpful ideas to consider when you make flying origami. First, prepare 2 pieces of paper of the same size. Fold one of them up tight and then drop them both at the same time. The folded one lands first, doesn't it? If you fold paper so as to put the center of gravity in just the right spot for gliding, it will fly. To make origami planes that fly well, please see my book "Flying Bird Origami," published by Seibundo Shinkosha.

As everyone knows, the way a see-saw or teeter-totter can balance on a narrow stick is a simple matter of center of gravity placement. A crane that is made from a few layers of paper is heavier than one made from just one sheet, even if it looks the same from the outside. With that in mind, I connected cranes to make the Crane Balancing Toy on page 69. You can apply this to other themes, too. For example, how about making a balancing toy with both adult and baby monkeys?

Supersonic Jet

1

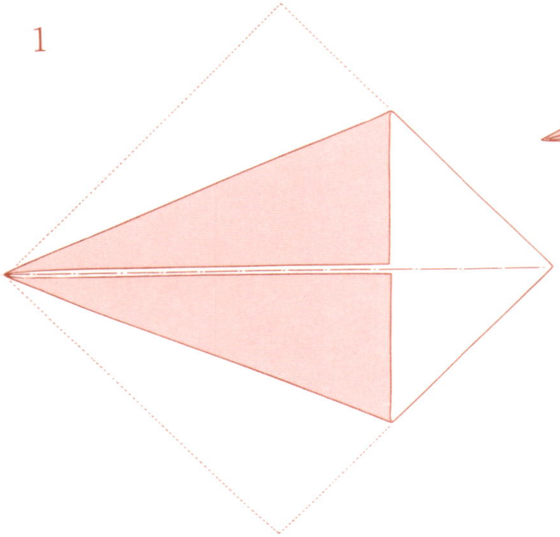

5

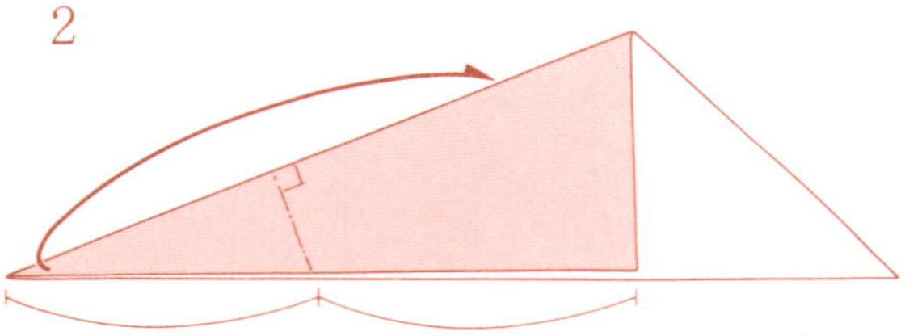

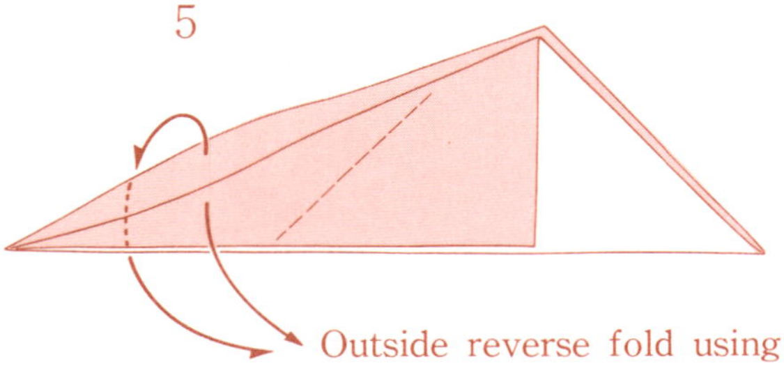

Outside reverse fold using
crease from step 3

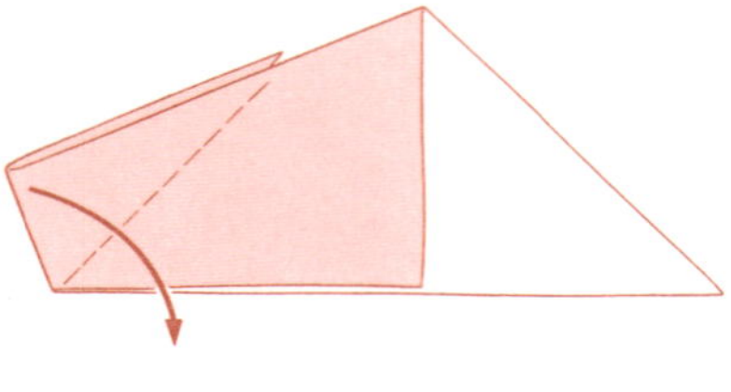

6

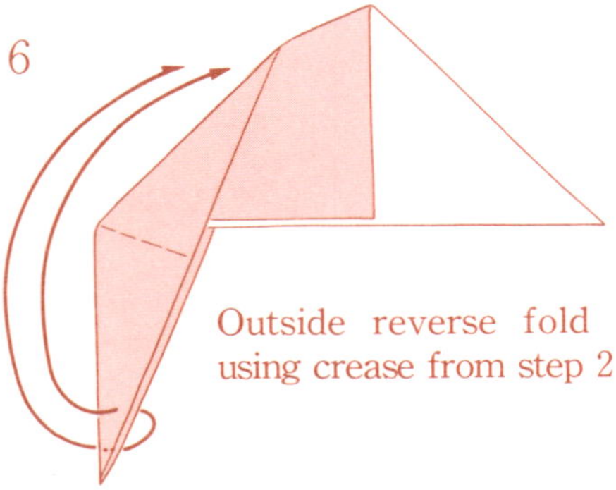

Outside reverse fold
using crease from step 2

2

3

7

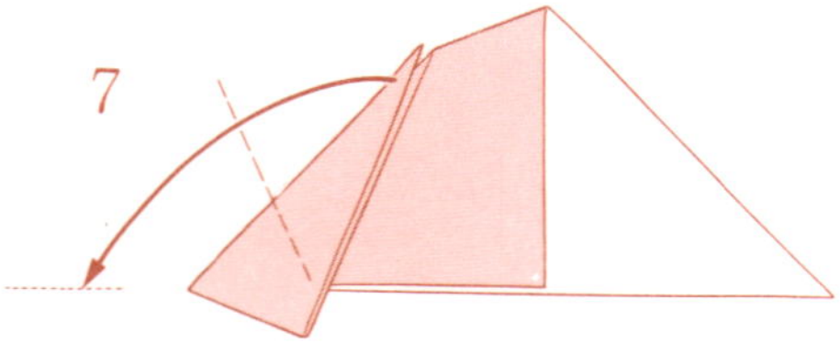

Outside reverse fold using
crease from step 4

4

8

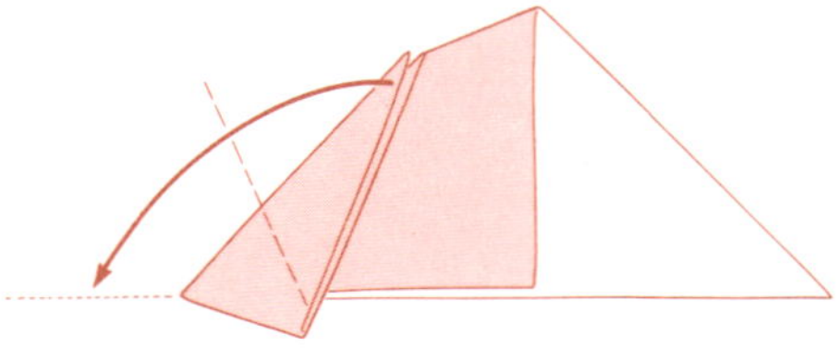

Make all folds to here then return
shape to step 2

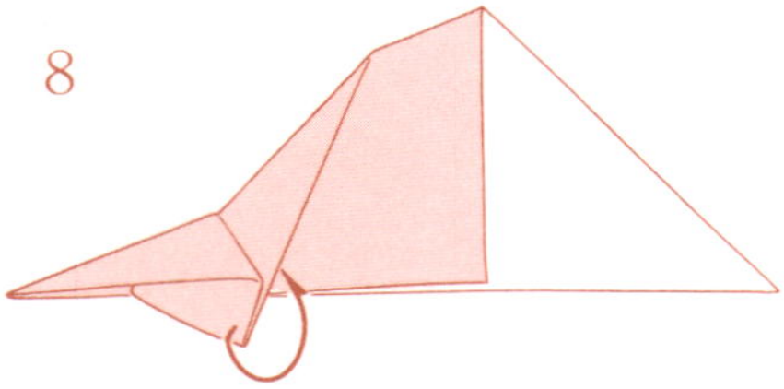

Fold up inside

9

Unfold just one layer from the middle

10

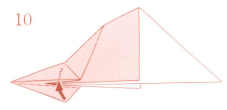

Fold up inside the gap shown to keep point from opening

11

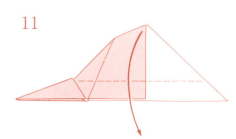

12

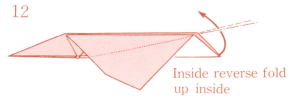

Inside reverse fold up inside

13

14

Finished

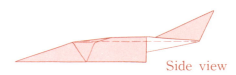

Side view

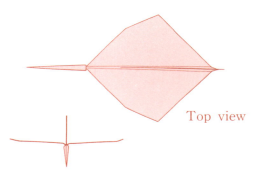

Top view

Front view

Jet Plane

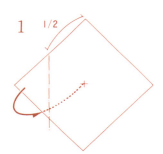

1   1/2

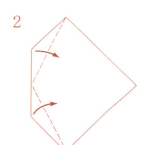

2

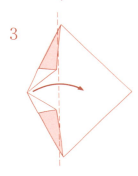

3

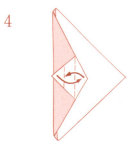

4

Diagram enlarged from here

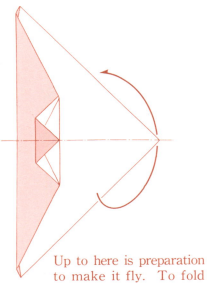

5

Up to here is preparation to make it fly. To fold just for the shape, you can fold from a triangle, but it will be without a front wheel.

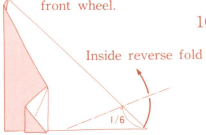

6

Inside reverse fold

1/6

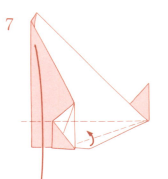

7

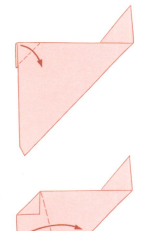

8

9

Fold across, opening triangle

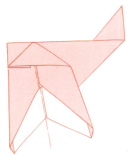

10

Fold other side open too

11

Enlarged from here

58

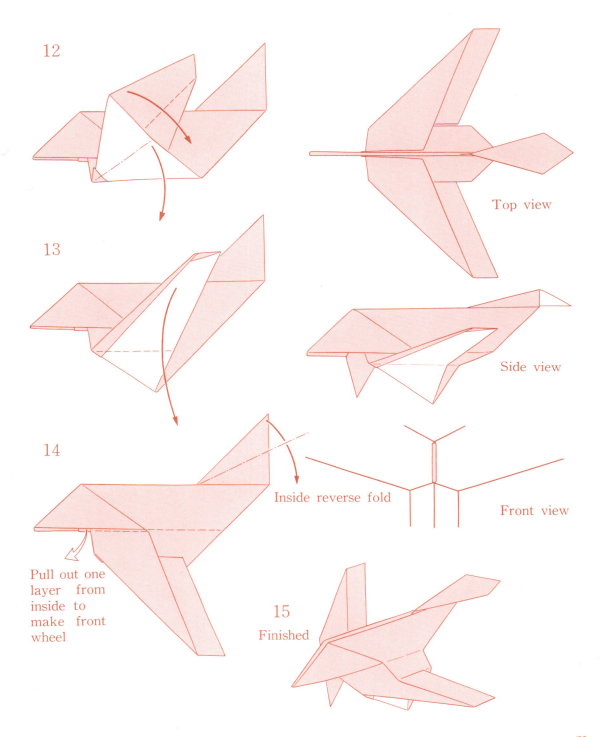

12

13

14

Pull out one
layer from
inside to
make front
wheel

Top view

Side view

Inside reverse fold

Front view

15
Finished

Flying Butterfly

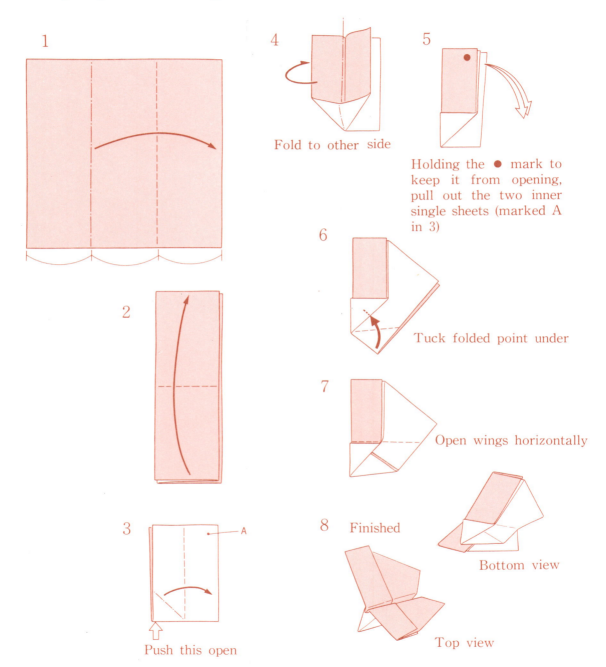

1

2

3

A

Push this open

4

Fold to other side

5

Holding the ● mark to keep it from opening, pull out the two inner single sheets (marked A in 3)

6

Tuck folded point under

7

Open wings horizontally

8 Finished

Bottom view

Top view

Swimming in the Wind Fish (mobile)

Attach these fish to thread and sticks to make a mobile. Faced into the wind of an electric fan, they will swim meanderingly through the air.

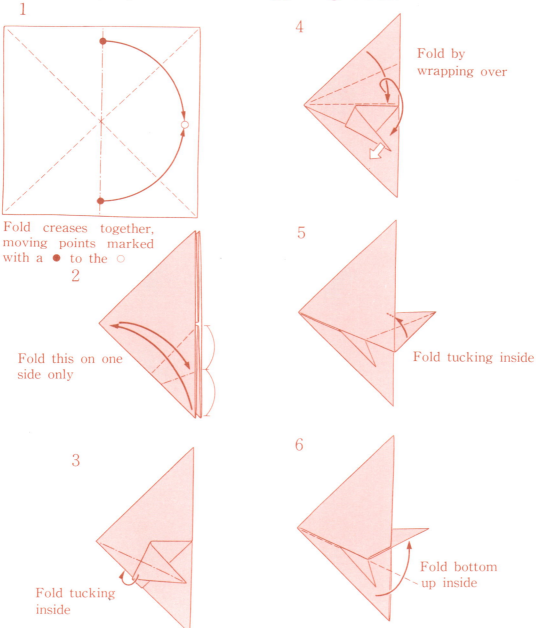

1

Fold creases together, moving points marked with a ● to the ○

2

Fold this on one side only

3

Fold tucking inside

4

Fold by wrapping over

5

Fold tucking inside

6

Fold bottom up inside

7

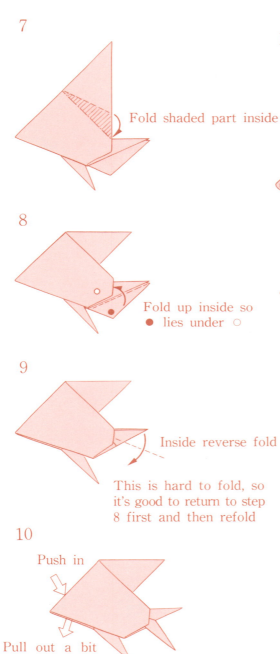

Fold shaded part inside

8

Fold up inside so
● lies under ○

9

Inside reverse fold

This is hard to fold, so
it's good to return to step
8 first and then refold

10

Push in

Pull out a bit
here to add bulk

Using a narrow needle, attach about
a foot of thread to hang.

11

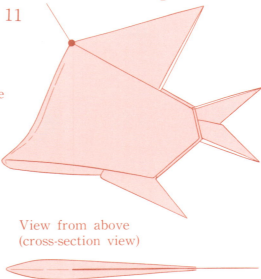

View from above
(cross-section view)

If you hang it in front of an electric
fan, it will sway back and forth in
the breeze, like it's swimming in
the wind.

Birds That Fly With Flapping Wings

It is possible to make origami birds that fly like paper planes. If you are interested in this, please read "Flying Bird Origami," issued by Seibundo Shinkosha.

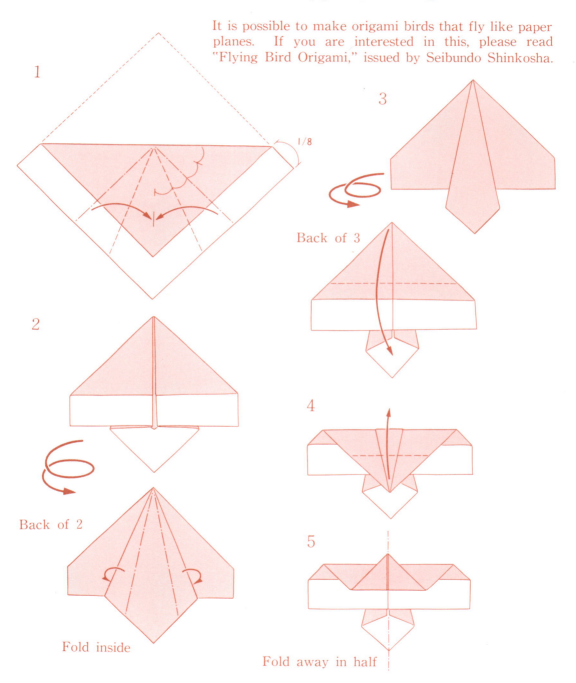

1

1/8

2

Back of 2

Fold inside

3

Back of 3

4

5

Fold away in half

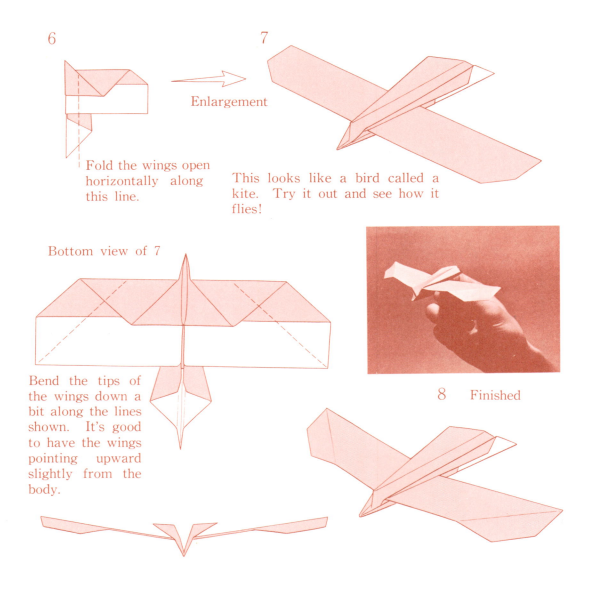

6

Fold the wings open
horizontally along
this line.

Enlargement

7

This looks like a bird called a
kite. Try it out and see how it
flies!

Bottom view of 7

Bend the tips of
the wings down a
bit along the lines
shown. It's good
to have the wings
pointing upward
slightly from the
body.

8   Finished

Folded as shown here, this bird lightly flaps its wings as it flies. However, since
wing flapping uses up some flight power, it may actually fly better without it.
The smaller the paper, the less the wings will flap. It's good to fold the wingtips
down about 15 degrees.

Papier Mâché Tiger

This is an origami version of the papier mâché tigers found at winter festivals in Japan. Make it with the 2 rectangular pieces of a square paper cut in half.

How to fold the neck

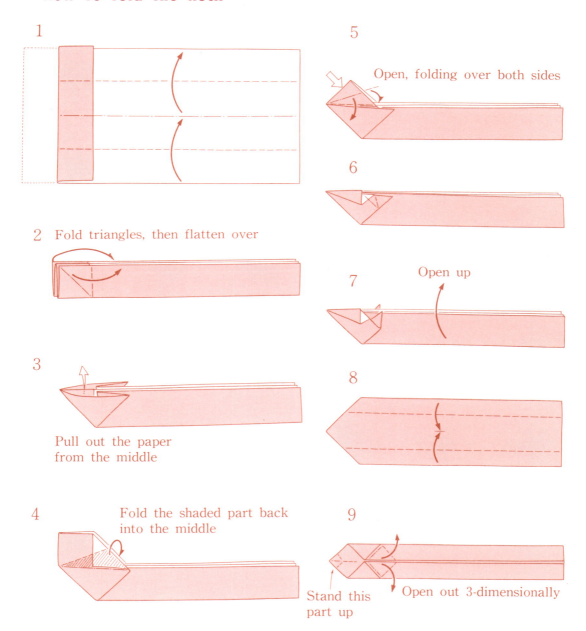

1

2 Fold triangles, then flatten over

3 Pull out the paper from the middle

4 Fold the shaded part back into the middle

5 Open, folding over both sides

6

7 Open up

8

9 Stand this part up   Open out 3-dimensionally

10

Tuck inside   Fold in half

14

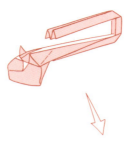

Tip of tail

Pull inside
paper down   This inner part
only is crinkled

11

Top view of 11

Outside reverse fold

Fold tail from here

12

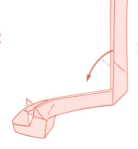

Inside reverse fold

15

This is the
fulcrum point

13

Finished neck and tail

66

Making the torso

1

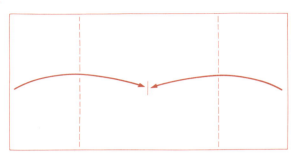

2

3

Inside reverse fold

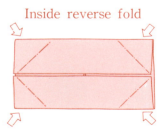

4

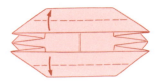

Open out from center

Mid-step

Fold in from
right and left

5

Return to step 4 and pull
out paper from inside

6

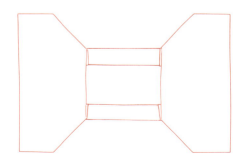

Back of 6

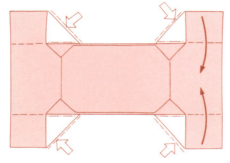

Make inside reverse folds to corners with thick arrows

7

8

 Turn over

9

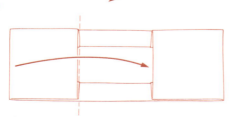

10

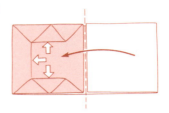

Spread open at white arrows to form box shape. Fold right half across and open it to box shape too.

11

Fold layered areas again along creases

12

Spread out to cylindrical shape, insert the neck from page 66 and it's finished!

13

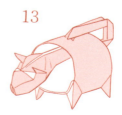

Crane Balancing Toy

This origami's center of gravity is the same as the doll's support point. It has unexpected properties, like the two small cranes being heavier than the big one.

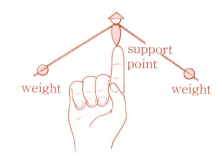

weight   support point   weight

1

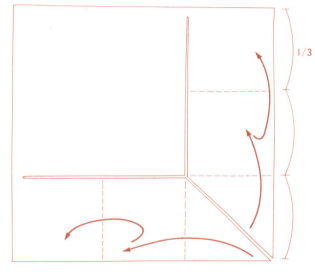

1/3

Cut as shown on the left, then fold up following the arrows.

3

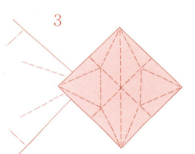

Position paper like this to fold small cranes.

2

neck   wing   wing   neck   tail   wing

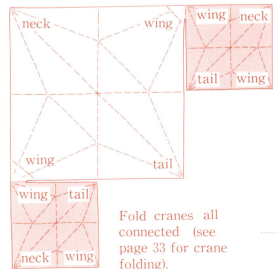

wing   tail   wing   tail   neck   wing

Fold cranes all connected (see page 33 for crane folding).

4   Finished

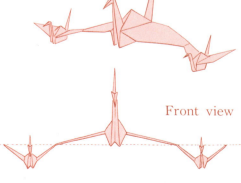

Front view

About the author: Yoshihide Momotani

Yoshihide Momotani graduated in 1952 from Kyoto University with a B.Sc. in botany. After completing the liberal arts assistant professorship program at Tezukayama University, he became a professor in biological science at University of Osaka Prefecture, where he taught until taking early retirement from the university in 1992. He continues to teach molecular biology at Phillips University Japan. He has a Ph.D. in Science, is a pharmicist, a member of the Japanese Botanical Society, a member of the Bio-Physics Society and president of Origami International Japan (address: c/o The Momotani Family, 30-5, Noda 3-chome, Kuzuha, Hirakata-shi, Osaka-fu, 573 Japan). His origami creations have been published in the Asahi Newspaper since 1970 and in the Sankei Newspaper since 1974, and information about his origami work was broadcast on Asahi TV in 1973 and on NHK TV in 1974. Exhibitions of his original works have been held in many countries over the past decade, 3 to 5 times a year, including both large and small displays. The most recent large exhibition was held at the International Youth Library in Munich in 1991. In the case of his exhibitions held in Japan, a section is sometimes devoted to the works of overseas origami enthusiasts.

A book of Professor Momotani's original origami works was first published in 1971, and since then 22 other such books have been released. Although his many readers around the world cannot read Japanese, they fold his origami models by following the diagrams in his books. This new text is a complete translation of the 1986 revised edition of the book first published in 1977 by Seibundo Shinkosha Publishing Co., Ltd.